THANKS FOR GIVING

ALSO BY KEVIN LORING

*Where the Blood Mixes**

* Published by Talonbooks

Thanks for Giving

A PLAY BY

Kevin Loring

TALONBOOKS

Talonbooks
278 East First Avenue, Vancouver, British Columbia, Canada v5T 1A6
talonbooks.com

Talonbooks is located on xʷməθkʷəy̓əm, Sḵwx̱wú7mesh, and səl̓ilwətaʔɬ Lands.

First printing: 2018

Typeset in Arno
Printed and bound in Canada on 100% post-consumer recycled paper

Interior and cover design by Typesmith
Cover painting, "Transformer" by Monique Hurteau. moniquehurteau.com

Talonbooks acknowledges the financial support of the Canada Council for the
Arts, the Government of Canada through the Canada Book Fund, and the Province
of British Columbia through the British Columbia Arts Council and the Book
Publishing Tax Credit.

Rights to produce *Thanks for Giving,* in whole or in part, in any medium by any
group, amateur or professional, are retained by the author. Interested persons are
requested to contact him care of Talonbooks: info@talonbooks.com.

Thanks for Giving was developed as an Arts Club Theatre Silver Commissions Project.

LIBRARY AND ARCHIVES CANADA CATALOGUING IN PUBLICATION

Loring, Kevin, 1974—, author
    Thanks for giving : a play / Kevin Loring.

ISBN 978-1-77201-218-7 (SOFTCOVER)

    I. Title.

PS8623.O743T53 2018   C812'.6   C2018-903447-5

I dedicate this work to my family and to the people of the N'lakapamux Nation.

PLAYWRIGHT'S PREFACE

The Thanksgiving holiday can be a complicated prospect for Indigenous families. On the one hand the celebration and coming together of the family is relished, while at the same time this holiday in particular is a stark reminder of the colonial traumas and genocides that have been inflicted upon Indigenous families since the settlement and colonization of Turtle Island.

At its core this play is about trauma, resilience, and legacy. The siblings John and Marie survived the loss of their father in a tragic accident that injured their mother, Sue, who has struggled with drugs and alcohol throughout their lives. Their cousin, Clayton, has survived as an orphan after the loss of his father in the same accident that took Marie and John's father; abandoned by his mother, he was raised by Nan, as John and Marie were. A Survivor of the residential school system, Nan has lost her son and has had to raise all of her grandchildren. Sam has had to survive the trauma of coming out to a family that has struggled to accept her queerness. Even Clifford has had to survive a sadistic father, as is revealed in the story about his dog. Sue is at once the most resilient and the most afflicted by trauma of the characters, having survived the accident that took her partner and twin brother, abuse by her stepfather, and substance addiction. Alongside these personal traumas is the male characters' involvement in ecological trauma, and, in John's case, in the traumas of war.

The Bear Dancer represents the matriarchal ancestor of Nan's family. And in many ways this play is about the resilience of her surviving spirit within this family. Though the killing of a bear in many rural communities is commonplace, for this family, because of their ancestral connection to the spirit of the Bear, it is like an assault. It represents, to me, the murder of the matriarchal spirit by a patriarchal force embodied by Clifford. And her resurgence through the legacy of this family is representative of the resilience of that matriarchal spirit.

Clifford's suicide is due to his inability to face the consequences of his actions. Yet the legacy of those actions lives on within the family in tangible ways. His memory haunts them and can only be exorcised by being confronted. Yet, as do all deaths, his leaves a hole – he cannot be directly confronted, and it is up to the survivors to find their way and make their peace without him. Sue's resurgence is the ultimate victory of the Bear spirit. In Sue and in Marie the family will find new matriarchs for its next generation.

—KEVIN LORING
AUGUST, 2018

THANKS FOR GIVING

PRODUCTION HISTORY

Thanks for Giving was first produced by the Arts Club Theatre in Vancouver, British Columbia, from October 5 to November 4, 2017, with the following cast and crew:

NAN	Margo Kane
CLIFFORD (Pa)	Tom McBeath
SUE	Andrea Menard
MARIE	Tai Amy Grauman
JOHN	čaačumḥi – Aaron M. Wells
CLAYTON	Deneh'Cho Thompson
SAM	Leslie Dos Remedios
BEAR DANCER	Shyama-Priya
Director	Kevin Loring
Set Designer	Ted Roberts
Costume Designer	Samantha McCue
Lighting Designer	Jeff Harrison
Sound Designer	James Coomber
Dramaturge	Rachel Ditor
Stage Manager	Angela Beaulieu
Assistant Stage Manager	Colleen Totten

CHARACTERS

NAN   an Indigenous grandmother, in her sixties
CLIFFORD (Pa)   Nan's husband (Caucasian), in his sixties
SUE   Nan's daughter, in her forties
MARIE   Sue's daughter, in her twenties
JOHN   Sue's son, in his twenties
CLAYTON   Sue's nephew, in his thirties
SAM   Marie's girlfriend (Asian)
BEAR DANCER

Act One

SCENE 1: THE BEAR MOTHER

The BEAR DANCER is revealed. She is wearing a Bear Robe and sitting on her haunches up centre. The BEAR DANCER crawls downstage towards the audience throughout the voice over.

NAN

(*voice-over*) When the Creator made the world it was the Bear that helped teach the First People how to live on the land. She showed them which foods to eat. When to eat them. Where to find it. Which medicines to use. And when to use them. We should always respect the Bear. She is our relation. You never know when you'll need her medicine. You never know if she will turn on you. You never know …

BEAR DANCER is strong, powerful, and fearless. She stands.

Gunshot.
Blackout.

SCENE 2: HUNTERS 1

Lights up. CLIFFORD has shot the Bear Mother. CLAYTON and JOHN are hunting with him.

CLIFFORD
Bear! Bear! Great big grizzly! I hit it!

CLAYTON
  Did it charge you?

CLIFFORD
  It's a fucking grizzly bear! It stood up and looked right at
  me. Christ. I'm still shaking.

JOHN
  We must have spooked it out to you.

CLIFFORD
  Yup. Prob'ly. I wounded it pretty bad.

JOHN
  Any cubs?

CLIFFORD
  Didn't see any. You can see where I hit it. Follow the
  blood. Dark blood. I hit it good.

    JOHN goes to the edge and looks down.

CLAYTON
  There's a wounded grizzly over there?!

CLIFFORD
  Just there in the brush.

    *CLAYTON loads his gun and approaches the
    ledge as well.*

CLAYTON
  I see it.

CLIFFORD looks out over the ledge. He raises his rifle. JOHN raises his rifle up.

CLIFFORD
    It's dead.

    The sound of bear cubs crying.

JOHN
    What's that? In the tree.

CLAYTON
    Cubs.

CLIFFORD
    Gotta shoot 'em.

JOHN
    What? Why?

CLIFFORD
    They'll die anyways. Winter's coming. We gotta shoot 'em. More humane if we shoot 'em now instead of letting 'em starve.

    CLIFFORD points his rifle up at the bear cubs in the tree.

CLAYTON
    Yeah but –

    CLIFFORD shoots.
    Blackout.

The echo reverberates across the
mountain valley.
Lights up. Music.

NAN is preparing a turkey dinner for her
family. While she prepares the feast, NAN
hums and sings a song.
SUE enters.

SUE
Have you heard from them yet?

NAN
I would have told you.

SUE
Just checking.

NAN
Did you manage to get to the store?

SUE
Not yet.

NAN
Well when you go for smokes ... I need these.

NAN hands SUE a list.

My lotto tickets. Oh and salad dressing.

SUE
Okay.

NAN
My purse.

> *SUE takes her mother's purse from the table
> and goes to exit.*

You don't need to take my purse. You don't need to
take my wallet. You're only going to the store. Just
take the money.

SUE
Okay. Okay.

> *SUE takes the money and leaves the purse and
> wallet on the table. She goes to exit.*

NAN
(*elbow deep into a turkey*) Well put my wallet back inside
my purse. And don't just leave it out on the table like that.
I need space for the food. I'm up to my elbows in turkey,
for Christ's sake!

SUE
Okay-okay.

> *SUE returns to the purse. She steals her
> mother's bank card from the wallet, returns the
> wallet to her mother's purse, and then puts the
> purse away. SUE exits.*

NAN
Whipped cream!

SCENE 3: HOMECOMING

*MARIE and SAM enter the kitchen. Nan
is offstage.*

MARIE

I'm nervous.

SAM

I should be the one who's nervous. They're your family.

MARIE

Exactly. You don't know what you're in for. Listen,
if my brother or cousin say anything awkward or
stupid, it's because they're awkward and stupid, don't
take it personally.

SAM

Got it. I brought a little treat for us. To take the
edge off a bit.

*SAM pops a drug-laced treat into her mouth.
She gives the other half to MARIE.*

MARIE

Pot brownies?! Are you crazy? You want to be high
through this experience?

SAM

Maybe later? It'll be an adventure.

MARIE

You are crazy.

MARIE goes to kiss SAM. NAN enters.

NAN
Oh hello dear! You made it!

NAN and MARIE embrace.

MARIE
Nan, this is my, uh, this is Sam.

NAN
Your roommate! Welcome! Take your coat off. Stay a
while, we don't bite, at least not until dinner.

SAM
Thank you. We brought you some wine. Marie said it's
your favorite.

NAN
How sweet of you.

MARIE
And we brought this too.

> *MARIE hands over a grocery bag with a
> tofurkey in it.*

NAN
What is this?

MARIE
Tofurkey.

NAN
That's obscene.

MARIE

We don't eat meat remember? Just fish.

SAM

And tofu.

NAN

Oh. Right. (*pause*) What am I supposed to do with this?

SAM

Just pop it in the oven for an hour.

NAN

Okay. Just pop it in the oven?

MARIE

Nan, it's just tofu. It's not going to explode. Where is everyone?

> *NAN puts the bag of tofurkey on the table or counter like it is toxic waste.*

NAN

The boys are out hunting. They've been gone all morning; I hope they bring me back a fresh liver.

SAM

Oh. Okay. Of what?

NAN

Deer, moose, or whatever. You know, in the old days, the old-timers would take out one of the gall bladders and cut it open and squeeze the yellow bile out onto a fresh liver like mustard and eat it just like that.

SAM
Wow.

MARIE
Gran!

NAN
It's true.

MARIE
Yeah but for Thanksgiving?

NAN
Well no … can you imagine, though. I can't even eat sushi.
Makes me gag. You eat that, raw fish?

SAM
Me? Oh yeah. I love it. We both do.

NAN
You too?

MARIE
Yeah Nan. Everyone does. It's sushi.

NAN
Not me. Fish head soup, that's another story. I just love
eating those eye balls.

MARIE
Nan!

NAN
Been up since five getting everything prepped for dinner.
There's still lots to do and here I am just a bitchin' in the

kitchen … Make yourself at home, Sam. Marie, show her the town. The big metropolis.

NAN exits.

SAM
Wow. She's awesome.

MARIE
Right?

SAM
She reminds me of my Grandma.

MARIE
She's everyone's Grandma.

SAM
She almost caught us.

MARIE
I know. Close call.

SAM
I feel like a teenager all over again.

MARIE
I'm sorry.

SAM
It's fun. Being a sneaky roommate. For now. But sooner or later.

MARIE
I know.

SAM

Let's live in the light.

MARIE

Come on, I want to show you my home town.

SAM and MARIE exit.

SCENE 4: HUNTERS 2

*CLIFFORD, CLAYTON, and JOHN drag
the Grizzly Mother to the truck. CLIFFORD
is holding a bloody plastic bag containing bear
parts: the bladders of the bears and the heart
of the mother.*

CLIFFORD

I used to come up here on horses. Used to be about a
dozen of us. Took us two full days' ride to get all the way
up here. No roads, just the old Indian pack trails. We'd
camp up here for about two weeks, get all our game and
then two days' ride back down to the trucks.

CLAYTON

Sounds like a good time.

CLIFFORD

We were a band of outlaws. Cowboys and Indians.
Literally. We had two pack horses just for booze.

JOHN

Now that's a hunting party.

CLIFFORD

The good old days. Two days' ride from town. This was our
video game. The mountains. Nobody walking around with
shit sticking out of their faces or holes in their ears as big
as beer cans. Jesus Christ! I never thought I'd see the day
where shit sticking out of your face was considered cool.

CLAYTON

I think it looks pretty badass.

JOHN

That's just human nature. Kids like sticking pins
in themselves.

CLIFFORD

If that's human nature, we're doomed.

JOHN

Marie calls it neotribalism.

CLIFFORD

Anyone calls themselves a neo-anything is pretty much
guaranteed to be a fuck-tard.

JOHN

Wow. That's creative.

CLAYTON

You know what pisses me off?

JOHN

I bet you're going to tell us.

CLAYTON
Green this and green that ... it's just a bullshit marketing
scheme. Global warming my ass. Sun's getting hotter.
That's it! That's all. Happens all the time. Same shit.
Different pile. It's natural. That's just the truth, how I see it.

CLIFFORD
Thanks for clarifying that for us.

> CLIFFORD guts the bear and begins removing
> organs. He takes out the heart and shows
> it to JOHN.

John, give me a hand. Look at the size of that heart.

> CLIFFORD puts the bear heart into a plastic
> bag with JOHN's help. CLIFFORD goes
> back to the gut pile and begins removing the
> gall bladder.

Speaking of veggie heads – (*glancing at his watch*) Your
sister should be home by now.

CLAYTON
She's bringing a friend. Her roommate? She's Asian
or something.

JOHN
Asian?

CLAYTON
Racist?

JOHN
No. How can I be racist? I'm part Native.

CLAYTON
Maybe your other parts are racist.

CLIFFORD
Do they even celebrate Thanksgiving?

JOHN
Why wouldn't they?

CLAYTON
They who?

CLIFFORD
The Chinese! Do they eat turkey? Did the Pilgrims
go there, too?

JOHN
I think the Chinese eat everything.

CLAYTON
The Pilgrims didn't invent turkey. The Indians
invented turkey.

CLIFFORD
What do you mean, the Indians invented turkey?

CLAYTON
The Pilgrims were starving and the Indians fed them. They
brought them a feast. They brought turkey.

JOHN
Cornucopias.

CLAYTON
Copious-cornholes.

JOHN
Exactly.

CLIFFORD
Baloney. The Pilgrims saved the Indians. Period.

Beat.

JOHN
She's probably just normal. Like us.

CLAYTON
Who you calling normal?

CLIFFORD
People are people. It doesn't matter if you're from an
inferior race or not.

CLAYTON
Wow.

JOHN
Damn. Captain Red Neck strikes again.

CLIFFORD
That's General Red Neck to you. Let's go. If we're late for
dinner, Nan will have our nuts for stuffing.

*CLIFFORD, CLAYTON, and JOHN gather
their gear and resume dragging the bear
carcass offstage to Clifford's truck.*

SCENE 5: GATHERER

SUE has some grocery bags with her.

SUE
What else was I supposed to get … lotto tickets, cigarettes. There's something else. Jell-O?

Her phone rings.

Shit. Hello?

NAN is revealed opposite to SUE, facing out to the audience, talking to SUE on her phone.

NAN
Don't forget the whipped cream!

SUE
I know, I know! What do you think? I am not an idiot. I got it.

NAN
The girls are here; hurry up.

SUE
Okay, okay.

She hangs up. Lights down on NAN. SUE remains.

Shit. Fuck.

SUE dials.

SUE
  Hello? Hey. Can you hook me up? I have to go to
  the bank machine first. Okay. Can you give me a ride
  home after? Okay.

    SUE hangs up. She pulls out her mother's
    bank card.

Whipped cream.

SCENE 6: JAM

    Lights up. MARIE enters the kitchen. NAN is
    prepping dinner.

MARIE
  Bannock!

NAN
  Fresh batch.

MARIE
  Got any jam, Nan?

NAN
  There's a huckleberry there. They were scarce this year,
  but I got some.

    MARIE retrieves a jar of jam from the fridge.

Did I tell you? I almost died.

MARIE
What?

NAN
I ran into a bear.

MARIE
Was he with his boyfriend?

NAN
What?

MARIE
Nothing.

NAN
I ran into a mother and her cubs.

MARIE
Where?

NAN
I was way up in the mountains. The High Stumps. That's
where they grow. Big patches of huckleberries. I was up
there all alone. Nobody wanted to come with me. I asked
your mom but she was too busy with whatever it is
she's up to. Anyways, that bear was way up on the ridge,
eating berries. I was just picking my first bucket when I
heard this roar –

MARIE
Jeez.

NAN

Great big grizzly bear. She caught wind of me. And I
thought, "Shit, I can't run. I'm too old." So I just kept
picking away. Then I heard her again. Way up. Crashing
around. Then all of a sudden, she roared and charged at
me. The bushes were going this way and that way … She
was coming at me full bore. All I could do was stand there
with my bucket of berries.

MARIE

Oh my god!

NAN

I thought, "That's it. Today is a good day to die."

MARIE

Well, obviously, it didn't eat you.

NAN

Nope she didn't.

MARIE

What did you do?

NAN

I started singing.

MARIE

To the bear?

NAN

I picked up these two rocks that were at my feet. And I
started banging them together like this, see, and I sang
to that bear.

*NAN grabs two pieces of bannock to use as
her stones and reenacts singing her song to the
charging Grizzly Bear. Banging her bannock/
stones together for percussion, NAN sings a
few bars of her Bear Song. This song should
resemble one of the wax cylinder Bear Songs
used in the sound design.*

NAN

Then she stops. Just there. On the ridge looking at me. Her
mouth all frothy from running down the mountain. She
stood up and looked right at me. Pawing the air, like this ...
Then I saw. She had cubs with her. Little fur balls following
after her. They were bawling for her. She turned on her
haunches and up she went. Back up the ridge to her babies.

MARIE

You banged rocks and sang a song to a charging grizzly
bear?! Can you be a little more Native?!

NAN

The hairs on the back of my neck were standing straight up,
I tell you. It was like there was electricity along the edges
of my skin. Even in the air between us. My heart was
beating so hard. She must have liked my song. She walked
away and left me alone. There was plenty of berries for the
both of us anyway.

MARIE

You're lucky to be alive!

NAN

I'm so old. She might as well have eaten a couch. I filled
my buckets and then back down the mountain. Made
about a dozen jars of jam. Froze the rest.

MARIE
You almost died to make this jam?

NAN
That's real good jam.

SCENE 7: FIRST CONTACT

> *JOHN, CLAYTON, and CLIFFORD return from hunting. There is blood on their hands. JOHN is carrying a bag of bear organs.*

JOHN
Never had bear before.

CLAYTON
Kinda sweet. Like wild boar maybe. You ever see one skinned?

JOHN
No.

CLAYTON
It's freaky. Looks like a person. Like a giant.

> *JOHN pulls the bear heart out of the bag and examines it.*

JOHN
Wonder what eating a bear heart will do?

CLAYTON
Nan would say it'll make you mean.

JOHN
    Really? Cool.

        JOHN returns the bear heart to the plastic bag.

CLIFFORD
    Remember what I told you. Don't tell your Nan. And
    wash your hands.

CLAYTON
    You don't think she's going to notice a grizzly bear hanging
    behind her shed?

CLIFFORD
    Just let me deal with it.

        CLIFFORD heads into the house. CLAYTON
        and JOHN head into the backyard.
        CLIFFORD encounters SAM in the kitchen.
        She has piercings.

SAM
    Oh hi. I'm Sam.

        SAM approaches CLIFFORD to shake his
        hand. CLIFFORD reveals that his hands are
        covered in blood. SAM recoils her hand.

CLIFFORD
    Uh huh.

SAM
    What's your name?

CLIFFORD
    Clifford. The kids call me Pa.

SAM
Okay. What should I call you?

CLIFFORD
Clifford.

SAM
Oh. Okay.

CLIFFORD
You're friends with Marie?

SAM
Yeah. I am.

CLIFFORD
You see Nan in there?

SAM
She's lying down, I think.

CLIFFORD
Is she? Good. Okay. Well. I got to wash up ...

SAM
Okay.

> CLIFFORD *exits to wash his bloodied hands,*
> *leaving* SAM *alone in the kitchen.*

Nice meeting you.

> SAM *exits.*

SCENE 8: GARBAGE

JOHN and CLAYTON are in the backyard hanging the bear behind the shed. They drag the bear carcass onto the stage, up center. They attach the front limbs to a large beam that is attached to a winch. The bear carcass is enormous and very heavy.

JOHN
Been thinking about school.

CLAYTON
Yeah?

JOHN
Thinking about doing something different.

CLAYTON
What are you going to take up?

JOHN
Something better than driving truck like you, anyways.

CLAYTON
Shit. Nothing wrong with driving truck.

JOHN
You driving that stink truck through town all the time. People are getting mad.

CLAYTON
Who?

JOHN
 Everyone.

CLAYTON
 That job pays good money.

JOHN
 Yeah.

CLAYTON
 Who was it that was getting mad?

JOHN
 Everyone.

CLAYTON
 Oh.

JOHN
 It stinks.

CLAYTON
 Yeah. Well. It's compost from the cities. Of course it stinks.
 All the yuppies and tree huggers think they're doing a
 solid for Mother Earth by composting, but really all
 they're doing is shipping their problem out here.

JOHN
 Don't you mean *you're* shipping it out here?

CLAYTON
 When I drive through town, everyone gives me the stink
 eye. Like I just shat on their faces.

JOHN

Somebody's gotta be that prick. Might as well be you.

CLAYTON

If Pa wants to shoot bears he should come out to the
Stink Farm. Haven't seen any grizzlies but there's always
black bears running around. And you should see the rats.
A gazillion rats crawling over acres of food scraps. I shit
you not, some of them are as big as dogs.

JOHN

How can you stand it?

CLAYTON laughs.

CLAYTON

They pay me better than anywhere else around here. Not
as good as oil-patch money, but it's work.

JOHN

Thought you were a high roller there. What happened?

CLAYTON

Blew it. Blew it all.

JOHN

Jesus.

CLAYTON

Easy come, easy go. We used to joke about how we're
raping Mother Earth. But damn, does raping Mother
Earth pay good! I had all the toys. Big truck, fast car,
Ski-Doo, ATV, wicked boat. Price of oil took a dive.

I got laid off. Eight months later, it was all gone. I was financed to the tits. Didn't save a penny. Nursing a pretty decent coke habit too. Helped with my drinking.

JOHN
How so?

CLAYTON
The more I did, the more I could drink!

JOHN
Damn.

CLAYTON
Fuck it. And fuck them if they don't like the smell of my stink truck. No one else is hiring! Work is work and that work pays good. So they can kiss my ass or find me a job that pays better.

JOHN
It's toxic. You're basically dumping stinking toxic shit onto the land.

CLAYTON
It's compost, idiot. It's green. Anyways, you can kiss my ass too. We don't all have brains around here.

> CLAYTON begins winching the bear carcass up into the air. It has been gutted but the head and fur remain intact. JOHN helps to stabilize the carcass to prevent it from swinging.

JOHN
I'm thinking about changing careers.

CLAYTON
Don't you have to have a career to change it?

JOHN
Never mind.

CLAYTON
You and Marie were always the bright ones. Me, I'll always be a laborer.

> *JOHN and CLAYTON finish raising the carcass into the air. It is back-lit by a work light. They step back to look at it. It dangles oddly, an ominous crucified silhouette. They look at it in awe.*

JOHN
Nan's going to be pissed.

SCENE 9: RITUALS OF THE FEAST

> *To music, the family sets the table. NAN pushes the dining table on stage, rolling it up centre and then, passing under the hanging bear carcass, down to centre stage. The other family members enter from all sides and place chairs around the round dining table, and then exit to return with place settings and food items that have been prepared for the feast. They place them on the table and then take their seats. NAN brings out the turkey and places it at the centre of the table. Everyone lets out an audible*

sound of excitement. SAM delivers the tofurkey
to the table and everyone is audibly disgusted.
The music ends. SUE is missing.

CLAYTON
Whoa! What the hell is that?

MARIE
Tofurkey.

CLAYTON
That's obscene.

MARIE
We don't eat meat.

CLAYTON
That's your problem. Pass the stuffing?

NAN
Hold on.

CLIFFORD
Where in the hell is Sue?

NAN
She went out for groceries earlier. Said she'd be
back later but ...

CLIFFORD
Well. No sense waiting for her. The food'll get cold. She
can have leftovers.

JOHN
Typical.

MARIE

She said she'd be here.

JOHN

Like I said, typical.

NAN

Put that down. We should pray before we eat. It's
Thanksgiving, for Christ's sake.

NAN stands and ALL bow their heads.

I give thanks to the Creator, for all that we have. I give
thanks to the earth for sustaining us. Thanks to the water,
the rains and the snow, the rivers and the lakes, and all
the fish in the seas and oceans. Thank you for their long
journeys home. I am thankful for the sun that warms us
and brings us the day. And I am thankful for the wind –

CLIFFORD farts.

CLIFFORD! Put a plug in it!

CLIFFORD

It was an accident.

NAN

Do you have to change your shorts?

CLIFFORD

No.

NAN

You sure?

CLIFFORD
Yes.

NAN looks at CLIFFORD.

I don't have to change my goddamn shorts! Now can we
eat please?!

NAN
Anyway. I am thankful for my family. Most of them.
My grandchildren. My stupid husband, and my – where is
she anyways? Sue? She should be back already. I ask you
to look out for her. Shine a light on her dark path. I am so
glad you are all here. All my relations.

ALL
All my relations.

NAN
Let's eat!

CLAYTON
Finally.

*ALL eat. SUE enters with grocery bags in
her hands.*

SUE
Oh just in time!

CLIFFORD
Here she comes. Boozy Susie.

NAN
I needed that stuff hours ago.

SUE
  I'm here now.

> ALL *dive into dinner. SUE is in really*
> *good spirits.*

Oh my babies are home. Look at them. Come here,
give me a hug.

NAN
  Better go wash up.

SUE
  Oh Mom, shush.

> *SUE goes over to MARIE and JOHN and*
> *hugs them each awkwardly as they sit at*
> *the table.*

NAN
  You smell like the bar. Go clean yourself up before you eat.
  I can't stand the smell of you.

SUE
  Alright, alright.

> *SUE exits to the bathroom. NAN follows.*

I told you I was just visiting with some friends.

NAN
  At the bar?

SUE mimes turning on the water. We hear the
sound of running water. SUE mimes washing
her hands and looking in the mirror.

SUE
  Just let me get cleaned up.

NAN
  Your eyes are all bloodshot. Put those drops in. You look
  like a damn pothead.

  SUE mimes turning the water off, and
  the sound of it pouring from the tap cuts
  out as well.

SUE
  Shut up, Mom. I'm not a pothead.

  NAN goes back to the dinner table, shaking her
  head. SUE makes sure she's gone. She pulls out
  a little baggy with white powder in it. She uses
  a key to dip into the baggy and snort a little
  bit of the powder. She quickly tucks the bag
  away. She then takes out some eye drops and
  puts them in her eyes. She looks in the mirror,
  readies herself, and then joins her family.

SCENE 10: FEAST

SUE enters. She sits down and they dish her in.

SUE
So how's everyone? How are you doing? Sam.

SAM
Yes. I'm good. Thank you.

SUE
Good. That's good. Hey! This is delicious!

NAN
Well try it first. You haven't even had a bite yet.

SUE
It looks delicious. I'm sure it's delicious.

SUE takes a bite.

SUE
I was right, delicious. Mom knows how to make a killer turkey dinner.

CLAYTON
Did you see Terry?

SUE
Gave me a ride home.

CLAYTON
Uh huh.

CLIFFORD
That guy is trouble. You should stay clear of him. Cops are watching that one. He's a goddamn criminal.

CLAYTON
Everyone's a criminal. Just depends on what you call a crime.

CLIFFORD
Wow. You should have been a lawyer.

> *ALL eat, trying to ignore how awkward the conversation is. SAM decides to try to offer up some conversation.*

SAM
This really is delicious.

SUE
Right?!

NAN
Thank you, dear.

SAM
You know Marie wrote a piece about Thanksgiving for her Native Studies class.

SUE
Really?! That's so cool!

CLAYTON
Oh yeah? Native Studies? Is that where they teach you how to be a Native?

MARIE

Yeah that's exactly what they teach you. Genius. No, we study the impact of colonialism and all the different atrocities and genocides across the Americas. It's intense. When you get past the sanitized version of history.

CLAYTON

Sounds like a good time.

CLIFFORD

Why would you want to dig all that up? It's beyond me.

MARIE

Seriously?

CLIFFORD

Seriously. Christ, we're still having to apologize for all the crap our ancestors did hundreds of years ago. Can't we just get on with it and live in the here and now?

CLAYTON

Pa is against everyone's history but his own.

NAN

It's good to look at where we've come from. How else are we going to know where we're going?

CLIFFORD

Look. We're all here. Celebrating. The harvest. Togetherness. Family. In the here and now. We don't need to rehash all the terrible shit people did to each other. Just be grateful for what you've got. Like the Pilgrims and the Indians from the original Thanksgiving.

MARIE
Which original Thanksgiving? There were many.

JOHN
Here we go.

CLIFFORD
The one where the Pilgrims and the Indians got together
and had a party.

SUE
Party!

MARIE
First European Thanksgiving Feast in Canada. 1578.
Martin Frobisher. British Arctic explorer. He was a pirate,
not a Pilgrim.

CLIFFORD
I know. I was in the navy.

MARIE
The Thanksgiving we're taught. The one where the
Pilgrims and the Natives shared their food, was actually
a feast to celebrate a raid on the Pequot. Seven hundred
men, women, and children were massacred.

SUE
Oh my god.

CLIFFORD
The Pilgrims killed seven hundred people?

MARIE

The Pequot were celebrating a harvest festival. They were
surrounded by English and Dutch mercenaries who
ordered them to come outside. Those who did were
shot or clubbed to death while the women and children
were burned alive inside the longhouses. Over seven
hundred people. That's twice as many as the massacre at
Wounded Knee.

CLIFFORD

Come on. The Pilgrims?!

MARIE

The Governor of the Colony declared "A Day of
Thanksgiving." And the Pilgrims had a feast. The heads of
the Indians they killed were kicked through the streets like
soccer balls. Maybe that's why there are so many Indian
Head mascots for sports teams. It's like burned into the
settler consciousness.

CLAYTON

You're such a buzzkill.

NAN

The *Europeans* didn't know their heads from their asses
when they came over here and the Natives were kind and
generous. And look what that got us. They shared their
food and they got beaten to death in return.

JOHN

Any more stuffing there?

NAN

Of course, dear.

MARIE
　Even the Wampanoag were attacked!

CLIFFORD
　The Wampa-who?

　　　JOHN turns to SAM. He indicates to MARIE.

JOHN
　Do you see what you've started?

SAM
　Who me?

MARIE
　The tribe from the legendary feast with the Pilgrims. One
　of their Chiefs was beheaded; they put his head on a
　pole – and left him like that, on display in the fort, for
　twenty-four years.

CLIFFORD
　Pretty brutal back then. In history.

CLAYTON
　Oh yeah? You having a memory?

SUE
　My baby is so smart. Both of them. I don't know where
　they get it from.

NAN
　Don't sell yourself short, dear. You're the artist
　in the family.

SUE

Thanks, Mom.

MARIE

Did you know they held feasts after every massacre?
And every time the churches would announce a day of
"Thanksgiving" to celebrate their victory over the "Savages"
in the promised land. The colonists attacked village after
village. Women and children were sold into slavery while
the rest were murdered. Boats loaded with Native slaves
were shipped to Europe –

CLIFFORD

Sure-sure-sure. And who helped them do these terrible
things? Other Indians.

SAM

First Nations?

CLIFFORD

Whatever. The other tribes were doing the same thing to
the colonists, to each other. Murdering, raping, slaving.
Those were just the times they lived in. You can't judge
it from our point of view. That doesn't make sense. The
world is soaked with the blood of the conquered.

> SUE *tries to divert the conversation to*
> *something more interesting.*

SUE

These potatoes are sure delicious, hey?

SAM

Mmm hmm so good.

NAN
It's all about the butter.

CLIFFORD
If I had a dime for every atrocity committed by some
group of people against another, I'd be a billionaire. It's
just human nature.

SUE
Mom, you really outdid yourself with these potatoes!

MARIE
Abraham Lincoln made Thanksgiving Day a legal
national holiday on the same day he sent his troops to
march against the Sioux who were starving in Minnesota.
So much for the Great Emancipator.

CLAYTON
The great pants invader?!

JOHN
Exactly!

CLIFFORD
But that's down in the States! It was different up here!

MARIE
We don't cross the border; the border crosses us.

JOHN and CLAYTON
Oh! Whoa!

SUE
Hey that's a song!

MARIE

And besides how different was it up here?! Just because the Americans slaughtered the Indians down there doesn't mean the same thing didn't happen up here. Canada was just passive-aggressive about their genocide.

CLIFFORD

Yeah well … that's history.

MARIE

The history we are taught to celebrate just glorifies the settlers and erases our struggles and experiences. It's just a total trumped-up, bullshit colonial narrative that serves to perpetuate the marginalization of Indigenous people and erase our history of continuous existence on this continent.

CLAYTON

Did you get all that?

CLIFFORD

I don't speak feminism. Can someone translate? What the hell is she saying?

JOHN

I thought they were Pilgrims, not settlers.

CLAYTON

You're a Pilgrim.

JOHN

Shut up, settler. You're always settling.

NAN

Both of you, settle down.

SUE
Good one, Mom.

CLIFFORD
Look the past is the past. We can't do anything about the
things we've done, all we can do is forget about the bad
shit and move on. So eat your tofurkey.

> CLIFFORD *reaches for more food. MARIE*
> *digs into her tofurkey. It's disgusting. She eats*
> *it, in defiance of its terrible taste. CLIFFORD*
> *enjoys a delicious morsel of Nan's fabulous*
> *turkey dinner.*

SUE
Isn't she so smart?

SAM
Yeah.

SUE
That's my baby. This one too. Isn't he cute.

JOHN
Mom.

SUE
What? It's true. I have such beautiful babies. Sam's cute
too. Do you have a boyfriend?

MARIE
Mom!

SUE
What? Am I embarrassing you?

JOHN and MARIE
  Yes!

NAN
  Sue. Cut it out. You're making our guest uncomfortable.
  It's good that you're learning all these terrible things dear.
  Pass the peas, please.

      MARIE passes the peas.

CLIFFORD
  Like I said, what's passed is past. All that matters is that
  the turkey is here and the potatoes are over there and the
  gravy boat is empty. Can someone pass those things this
  way? And will one of you find it in the kindness of your
  hearts to refill the gravy boat? Please and thank you.

      *CLIFFORD holds out the gravy boat to
      MARIE. MARIE takes the gravy boat and
      exits into the kitchen. The family all exhale
      and visibly relaxes once Marie has left the
      room. ALL eat.*

      NAN looks over to JOHN.

NAN
  What about you dear? How are you liking university?

JOHN
  Good. Real good. (*pause*) I quit.

      ALL stop eating. The shit has truly hit the fan.

NAN
  What?!

CLIFFORD
Say again?

NAN
No you didn't.

JOHN
I'm joining the army.

> NAN, CLAYTON, and CLIFFORD laugh.
> JOHN is serious. SUE looks at her son,
> concerned. The others stop laughing.

NAN
No you're not.

SUE
But you were so good at school. Remember all the awards
you got for being so smart. You and your sister. I was
never that smart.

JOHN
It's a career. You go in. They train you up. You can take all
kinds of courses in the army and they pay you. Which is
good. 'Cause we don't really have a lot of money. So –

NAN
I thought you had it all worked out. I thought you
liked school.

JOHN
I was bored. I hated it.

CLIFFORD
So you're joining the army?

MARIE

(*offstage*) You're joining the fucking army?!

CLAYTON turns to SAM.

CLAYTON

Now the shit has really hit the fan.

NAN

Why would you do that?

MARIE re-enters the dining room.

MARIE

You're an idiot!

CLIFFORD

Nothing wrong with serving your country. I did. Four years in the navy.

CLAYTON

You know what they say about sailors.

CLIFFORD

There's a long history of Indians serving in the forces. They fought in every single war. Some of the most decorated soldiers are Indians.

SAM

First Nations.

CLIFFORD

Exactly.

JOHN

And if I want to go back to school, they'll pay for it.
It's a career.

CLIFFORD

Exactly.

MARIE

Killing people is a career?

JOHN

I want to serve my country. I thought you guys
would be proud.

MARIE

You really think this is your country?

CLAYTON

Hey man, don't listen to her. I'm proud of you. Congrats.

CLIFFORD

Me too. Congratulations. Good for you. I'm proud of you.
Go for it. You'll learn a lot, boy. They'll straighten you out.
Make you a man.

MARIE

You aren't man enough now? You need to join the army
to be a man?

CLIFFORD

He's signing up to protect your freedom.

MARIE

You're an Indian! Hello?! The army doesn't protect
Indians! The army kills Indians!

SAM
First Nations.

MARIE
I know. It's okay.

CLAYTON
He's not murdering anyone. He's joining to protect our
freedom. Which is more than you're doing. Sitting around
bitching about how deeply offended you are by everything.
Besides, you're part Pilgrim too.

MARIE
Are we really going to calculate our blood quanta right
now? Really? We grew up eating bannock sandwiches.

NAN
Hey! What's wrong with my bannock sandwiches?

CLIFFORD
I always liked your bannock.

NAN
Oh Clifford.

JOHN
Why do you have to act like you lived through the Indian
apocalypse all the time? You act like you were massacred
at Wounded Knee! We're not even from that part of the
world! Those aren't even our people. Those are some other
Natives. And here you are so hurt by what happened to
them on the other side of the continent 450 years ago.

MARIE
Today. Idiot. It's all still happening. Today. And why are
you such a fucking apologist? Are you ashamed?

JOHN
I got no shame.

MARIE
Are you ashamed that you're an Indian?!

SAM
First Nations.

MARIE, CLAYTON, JOHN, and CLIFFORD
Whatever!

NAN
Everyone shut up.

JOHN
You're such a dyke!

    CLAYTON squeals.

NAN
I said shut up! You're scaring our guest. And you're
spoiling my dinner that I slaved over all day for you
people to eat. Now no more fighting at my table. You
hear? We're here to be thankful for what we've got.

    ALL shut up.

I'm sorry dear. Are you okay?

SAM

I'm not sure actually. I think so.

CLAYTON

Why? Are you a dyke too?

NAN

Clayton!

CLIFFORD

Dammit Clayton. Don't be stupid.

MARIE

Actually we both are.

> *Everyone looks at MARIE, who reaches for*
> *SAM's hand. MARIE and SAM hold hands.*
> *SAM is embarrassed. MARIE is defiant.*

JOHN

Called it!

CLIFFORD

Oh for Christ's sake. Can't we just eat?

NAN

Enough.

CLAYTON

Is anyone actually surprised? Because, I'm not. Always
knew you were a pillow-biter.

MARIE

That's not even the right slur, you moron.

NAN

Clayton, shut up. You're insulting all of us with
your stupidness.

CLAYTON

Why's everyone ganging up on me?

MARIE

Because you're acting like an idiot.

CLIFFORD

He's not acting. He is an idiot.

CLAYTON

I'm an idiot? Wonder Boy here joined the army because
he was bored. This one here finally came out of the closet,
to the surprise of no one! And you. You're the one who
shot that grizzly. And those two –

CLIFFORD

You shut your mouth.

CLAYTON

Those Conservation Officers find out they'll be knocking
on the door. Again.

CLIFFORD

That damn grizzly charged at me!

CLAYTON

Oh yeah, now it was charging at you.

> CLAYTON *laughs.* CLIFFORD *pouts and*
> *stuffs his face with his dinner.*

SUE
You respect your elders.

CLAYTON
He's not my elder. He's just old.

CLAYTON *gets up unsteadily on his feet. The
whiskey has indeed been working on him for a
while. CLAYTON staggers out of the room.*

NAN
You shot a bear?

CLIFFORD
Grizzly. It was a grizzly. I had to. It was right on top of me.

NAN
Where?

CLIFFORD
High Stumps.

NAN *nods. A pained look comes over her.*

NAN
Did you see her cubs?

CLIFFORD
There weren't any.

NAN
She had cubs.

CLIFFORD
How in the hell do you know? We didn't see any
goddamn cubs.

NAN
Where is she?

CLIFFORD
Hanging. Out back.

NAN
You going to eat her?

CLIFFORD
It. It's a bear. It doesn't have a name.

NAN
Səxʷswcʷ tə Kże. That was her name. And she was a
good mother.

> NAN *gets up from the table and exits the*
> *room. ALL are taken aback by all that has just*
> *happened. ALL retreat to their dinner plates.*

SUE
Pie?!

> *Lights fade. ALL clear the table of the*
> *dinner, leaving only the pie and some plates*
> *and utensils.*

SCENE 11: TRICK OR TREAT

Lights up. SUE, MARIE, SAM, JOHN, and CLIFFORD are still in the dining room.

SUE brings Nan's homemade pumpkin pie to the table. She takes the whipped cream out and covers the top of the pie with a heaping mound of whipped cream.

MARIE and SAM feed each other pot brownies. They walk into the dining room.

JOHN
Who made this pie anyway?

SUE
Mom, of course.

MARIE
Who wants some?

CLAYTON staggers back into the room.

CLAYTON
I do.

MARIE and CLAYTON take bites of the pie at the same time. It is not the taste they were expecting.

Whoa! What the –

MARIE
It's so salty!

SUE
What?

MARIE
Try it!

She does.

SUE
Mom?!

CLAYTON
It's like she substituted salt for sugar!

MARIE
Maybe she mixed them up.

SUE
That's not like her.

NAN walks in.

NAN
How's my pie?

SUE
It's great. Right Clayton? Have another bite.

CLAYTON
What? No, I'm good.

SUE shoves another bite of pie into
CLAYTON's mouth.

SUE
  Mmm. Good, right?

  It's clearly not.

CLAYTON
  Mmm hmm ...

SUE
  More?

EVERYONE
  No thanks.

NAN
  What's wrong with it?

    NAN takes a bite of her pie. She
    smacks CLAYTON.

  Why did you put so much salt on my pie?

CLAYTON
  I didn't.

NAN
  You ruined it!

    SUE, MARIE, SAM, JOHN, CLIFFORD,
    and CLAYTON all laugh. NAN is angry and
    embarrassed.

CLIFFORD
Hey! Where's mine?!

NAN
Here.

> *NAN shoves a mouthful into CLIFFORD.*
> *He spits it out.*

CLIFFORD
What the hell is this? Are you trying to kill me?!

NAN
If I wanted to kill you, you'd never see it coming.

> *NAN exits.*

> *Transition to:*
> *SUE, MARIE, SAM, JOHN, CLIFFORD,*
> *and CLAYTON setting into the living room,*
> *forgoing dessert for more drinks.*

SCENE 12: MARIE AND SAM

> *SUE, MARIE, and SAM are in the kitchen.*
> *CLIFFORD sits in his chair.*

SUE
Hey ...

MARIE
Look, I know this is probably weird or whatever for
you. I just ...

SUE

Oh it's not that weird, really. I mean, I suspected …

MARIE

You suspected? Seems like everyone suspected.

SUE

So … Where did you two meet?

MARIE

At a bar.

SUE

Of course.

SAM

No. We were in the same class. She didn't even notice me.

MARIE

That's not true.

SAM

You ignored me the whole time.

MARIE

I was oblivious.

SAM

You're so cute when you're oblivious.

MARIE

Anyways I didn't know she was checking me out.

SAM
    She does this thing with her pen, when she's thinking
    about something.

MARIE
    What?

SAM
    You play with your lips with it.

MARIE
    What?

SAM
    You trace the edge of your lips with it.

MARIE
    So?

SAM
    I thought it was ...

MARIE
    What?

SAM
    Hot. Cute. Cute-hot.

MARIE
    You're funny.

SAM
    It's true.

MARIE
You never told me that before.

SAM
It's true.

MARIE
Anyways, I was oblivious. And we were at a club.

SAM
We danced together.

MARIE
Yeah.

SAM
I was like, "Hi there."

MARIE
Like a cheesy middle-aged man.

SAM
Your friends ditched.

MARIE
I was alone ... And she came home with me.

SUE
Oh. I see.

SAM
I walked her home.

SUE
That's it?

SAM
  And stayed the night.

SUE
  Oh.

MARIE
  Seemed like the right thing to do.

SUE
  Was it?

MARIE
  Yeah.

          NAN enters.

SUE
  Are you happy?

MARIE
  Yeah.

SUE
  Good. Me too then.

          CLIFFORD enters the kitchen.

CLIFFORD
  Happiness is overrated.

NAN
  You're telling me.

SAM

How did you two meet?

NAN

At the Remembrance Day Powwow.

CLIFFORD

I'd never been to a powwow before.

NAN

I saw this SOB standing in the crowd wearing a navy
uniform. And I says, "What the hell's he doing here?"

CLIFFORD

All these Indians, dressed up like Christmas.

NAN

Not like Christmas! And we're First Nations now,
or Aboriginal, or Indigenous. Not Indians. It's the twenty-
first century. Get your head out of your ass.

CLIFFORD

Back then you were Indians.

NAN

We were never Indians. Right Sam?

SAM

Right.

CLIFFORD

Yeah well she was the best-looking woman I had ever seen.
Indian–First Nations–Native–Indigenous–Aboriginal or
otherwise. Still is.

NAN
See. That's why I call him Walking Eagle. He's so full of shit he can't fly.

NAN exits.

SCENE 13: THE DOGS

SAM, MARIE, and CLIFFORD retreat to the living room. CLIFFORD sits in his chair. SAM and MARIE sit on an ottoman. CLIFFORD regards SAM for a long time.

CLIFFORD
So what do you do?

SAM
Me?

CLIFFORD
Well I know what she does, so what are you into?

SAM
Sound design. For video games. Mostly. I'm not working right now.

CLIFFORD
I thought you were going to school. With Marie –

SAM
I am. Part-time. I'm also a dog walker. For a little extra money?

CLIFFORD
Dog walker? You walk dogs?

SAM
Yeah.

CLIFFORD
People pay you?

SAM
Yeah.

CLIFFORD
I like dogs. 'Bout time to get a new one, but Nan
won't let me.

SAM
You don't strike me as a dog person.

CLIFFORD
Always had a dog. (*pause*) When I was a kid I used to
have this Black Lab that could climb trees just like a cat.

SAM
No way!

CLIFFORD
I'd put an orange floor-hockey ball in a tree and he'd
climb right out onto the limb to get it. I'd take him grouse
hunting. If I winged a grouse he'd catch that bird right out
of the air, trot back to me, and lay it at my feet. His teeth
would never even pierce the meat. Soft mouth, eh. He was
a damn good dog.

SAM
We have a dog.

MARIE
Duchess.

SAM
Pomeranian.

CLIFFORD
Rat balls!

SAM
I beg your pardon?

CLIFFORD
Don't like 'em.

MARIE
You don't like Pomeranians?

CLIFFORD
Nope. It was a Pomeranian that killed my Black Jack. Little
Pomeranian bitch was in heat; I think it belonged to one
of the nurses. Every dog in town was howling for this silly
little Pomeranian bitch. All night long. People couldn't
sleep. Back then, my Old Man was the mayor. One of the
jobs he made for himself was to round up all the strays in
town. If your dog was on the streets, he'd round them up
early in the morning. He'd put dog food in the back of his
truck, laced with antifreeze in case any escaped.

SAM
Oh my god!

CLIFFORD
Little ones, big ones. If it was on the street unaccompanied, collar or no collar, and it was the wrong day of the month, your dog was dead. He'd drive them up to the dump, and shoot 'em with this little .22 Magnum he had.

SAM
Oh my god. Why?

CLIFFORD
Strays were a real problem. Some kid got bit. Little girl got all tore up. So that was how they dealt with it. My old man, he kind of liked it. He was a veteran. Normandy, the whole nine yards. Well, that little Pomeranian bitch was in heat, tied up in her yard. Every mutt in town was howling, fighting, whining. My old man had enough. He jumped the fence and stole that stupid little bitch.

MARIE
Are we still talking about a dog?

CLIFFORD
Threw her in the back of the truck. Before long every loose dog in town was in the back of my old man's truck. Including mine.

SAM
What?

CLIFFORD
I thought he was in the yard. I forgot to tie him up. He jumped the fence. My old man picked him up on the street.

SAM
  Didn't he know that he had your dog?

CLIFFORD
  Oh he knew.

SAM
  Oh my god, I can't even deal ...

  CLIFFORD finishes his whiskey.

CLIFFORD
  I woke up the next morning and Black Jack was gone.
  My dad was already sitting at the table drinking his coffee,
  reading the paper. Black Jack's collar sitting there in
  front of him.

MARIE
  Nan! Grandpa's telling morbid stories!

NAN
  (*offstage*) Tell him to shut up!

MARIE
  Pa. Nan says shut up.

CLIFFORD
  Tell her never mind. Here. Go fill up my glass if you're
  going to whine.

  MARIE takes CLIFFORD's drink and exits.

CLIFFORD
  I begged him to bring Black Jack home. So I could bury
  him. But he wouldn't. So I rode my bike out to the dump.

Pulled him out of a pile of dead dogs. He was at the very bottom. Must have been the first dog he shot. I found a tree up on the hill there. Dug a hole and buried him.

SAM
How old were you?

CLIFFORD
Nine. Ten maybe.

SAM
That's so sad. I think I might vomit.

CLIFFORD
Don't know why I shared that. I don't usually share. Not with strangers. Must be the whiskey. Always brings out the darkness.

SAM
Maybe we're not strangers anymore.

CLIFFORD
(*grunting*) Don't be so sure.

SCENE 14: GRIZZLIES

NAN sits out back, drinking a glass of wine.
MARIE joins her.

NAN
  Oh hey.

MARIE
  Hey.

NAN
  So?

MARIE
  Surprised?

NAN
  I don't know.

MARIE
  Disappointed?

NAN
  No of course not. After my first husband died, and I was
  first dating Clifford, not everybody liked it. My friends,
  some of my cousins, they were like you. They believed in
  stuff. They wanted to fight and make a lot of noise. Didn't
  like me dating a *shAma*, a white man, you know. I thought
  he was handsome. A lot of good that did me. We had our
  hard times too, eh, over the years, but we got through it.
  Nowadays people can be whoever they want. It's not a big
  deal anymore, nobody cares. Nobody should.

MARIE

Thanks, Nan.

> NAN *takes a sip from her wine. She stares into it, looking back into the past.*

NAN

I had a friend at residential school. Brenda. She was from way up north. She was so lonely when she came here. She didn't know anyone. When Brenda first came here she would cry all night. And those nuns would get mad and punish her. Beat her with a strap, eh. One night Brenda started crying again. I crawled into bed with her and held her tight until she stopped, and she fell asleep. Then I got up and went back to my bed. Next night, when everyone was asleep, she came over to my bed and crawled in. We held each other like that all night. Just before morning, she got up and went back to her bed. And that's what we did. Every night. She'd come over and visit me, slip into my bed. We knew that we'd really get it if we got caught. Those nuns would kill us. We were just kids you know. As innocent as you could be in that scary place. We just needed someone. Someone to hold on to.

MARIE

I think Sam is more than that.

NAN

I know, dear.

MARIE

Why did you tell me that story?

NAN

It's not wrong to love. I just want you to be happy.

CLIFFORD enters.

CLIFFORD
Are you just going to leave this carcass on the table all goddamn night or is someone going to put it away?!

NAN
Put it away yourself!

CLIFFORD exits.

Ugh. Dumb-ass. I can't believe he went out and shot that bear. We're not even supposed to eat bear.

MARIE
Why not?

NAN
That's our ancestor. My mother would say that we are guided by the Bear.

MARIE
Really?

NAN
And you and your brother are grizzly bears.

MARIE
Huh?

NAN
The old people would say that when you had twins it meant that they are grizzly bears. There was a whole teaching around that. My mother had me brushed down with cedar boughs and they prayed over me after I had my

kids. When Sue had you two, my mother wanted to sing her Bear Song for you. But I never let her.

MARIE
Why not?

NAN
Well, I guess that residential school beat it out of me real good. A lot of stories and songs got beaten out of us, you know. I still get anxious just thinking about the old ways, let alone talking about them.

MARIE
You never told me that before.

NAN
Nobody ever shot a grizzly bear and hung it in my backyard before.

MARIE
I hate them for what they did to you at that school.

NAN
You make me brave. You're the one interested in history. So now you know.

MARIE
I'm going to have a Bear Clan coming-out party!

NAN
There is a funny story about the bear. One day there was this Chief's daughter who stepped in bear shit.

MARIE
  That's the legend? "The Woman Who Stepped
  in Bear Shit"?

NAN
  Just listen. She started complaining about how gross and
  dirty bears were for leaving their shit around. A grizzly
  heard her and transformed himself into a real handsome
  man. And seduced her.

MARIE
  That's like Native *Beauty and the Beast*.

NAN
  Anyways, they had two cubs together, twins, and they
  could all transform themselves into people and back into
  bears. At will. That's where we come from. We come from
  those bears.

MARIE
  Cool.

NAN
  You and your brother are grizzly bears. Just like your
  mom and uncle.

          NAN gets up and looks uneasily toward the
          shed in the backyard.

  Now we have a dead one hanging in the backyard.

MARIE
  What's he going to do with it?

NAN

He wants to eat it. He probably wants to stuff it like all
his other stuffed animals in the living room. I swear I can
barely go in there sometimes. It's like they're watching me.

MARIE

I've never had bear before. Have I?

NAN

I would never feed it to my kids. It'd be like eating one
of your relatives. My mother would say if you fed bear to
your kids it'll make them mean. That Bear Spirit would
be angry and live inside you ... But people eat bear. Back
in the old days more than now. Not everything that's
negative is bad you know. Maybe they needed that Bear
Medicine to be fierce.

SCENE 15: NEGOTIATION

*CLIFFORD is in his chair in the living room
on his phone. On the wall behind him are the
mounted heads and skins and stuffed animals
he's killed over the years. Trophies. There are
many. CLAYTON overhears the phone call.*

CLIFFORD

Yeah. Three. Two little ones and a big one. A hundred and
fifty bucks a gram for the gall bladders. You want the paws
too? Okay. We can negotiate that. I might have to go back
and get the little ones. If you want them I can get them.
Yeah. I just left them there. No. Don't lowball me. I could
get into a lot of trouble. So ... okay. Okay, sounds good.
See you then.

CLAYTON enters the living room.

CLAYTON
You're poaching bears for parts?

CLIFFORD
What the hell are you talking about?

CLAYTON
I know where there's bears.

SCENE 16: GARDEN

MARIE and NAN are still in the garden.
SAM enters. She's a bit cautious after all
that's happened.

SAM
I was just wondering where you were –

MARIE
It's okay, come here.

NAN
I warned you we might bite at dinner.

SAM
Yeah. You did.

MARIE reaches for SAM's hand. She takes it.

SAM
What are you guys doing out here?

NAN

I'm trying to get enough courage to go look at this bear that's hanging up behind my shed.

SAM

Oh. Right. Gross.

MARIE

I'm sorry. That's not how I imagined it would go.

SAM

I know. It's okay. Nobody seems to be too upset about it. So, Victory! It's better than what happened when I came out to my family.

NAN

What happened?

SAM

My father still won't talk to me. My mom will, but … it's just different.

NAN

I'm sorry, dear.

SAM

It's okay.

NAN

No it's not. That's family. Whether you like it or not, you're stuck with them. Might as well love 'em.

SCENE 17: BLACK SHEEP

SUE is playing the guitar. CLAYTON enters.

CLAYTON
Aunty.

SUE
Oh hey, Clay.

> *CLAYTON sidles up beside his aunt. He is
> drunk and sullen.*

You okay?

CLAYTON
I'm good.

SUE
Yeah?

CLAYTON
Quite the dinner, eh? Like a soap opera.

SUE
Can't choose family.

CLAYTON
Nope. Sure can't.

SUE
Mom sure knows how to make a feast though, eh?

CLAYTON
  Shit yeah.

SUE
  You sure you're okay?

CLAYTON
  Oh yeah. You know me.

SUE
  You can always talk to me. Okay?

CLAYTON
  Thanks, Aunty.

      CLAYTON puts his arm around SUE.

SUE
  'Course.

      *CLAYTON hangs his head. SUE stops playing
      and pulls a joint out from behind her ear.*

  I hope this shit isn't laced.

CLAYTON
  Ah that's just bullshit, nobody's lacing weed.

SUE
  I don't know. It's got quite a kick. Feels like you're in a
  music video. Everything just feels …

      CLAYTON laughs.

CLAYTON
   Thick and juicy, eh Aunty? Until we OD and die.

SUE
   Don't say that.

CLAYTON
   Want to go pay our respects?

       SUE takes the joint back. Considers it.

SUE
   Okay. I'll make a plate for them. They'll like that.

       Lights fade on them.

SCENE 18: EXILES

       *SAM and MARIE play hide and seek through
       the trees in the backyard. They catch each other,
       kiss, and begin to slow dance. JOHN sees them.*

MARIE
   Sorry about my mom.

SAM
   What for? She seems really sweet.

MARIE
   Come on. You don't have to pretend. She's so fucked up.

SAM
   Babe. Stop apologizing for your family.

MARIE

She is though. (*pause*) She was in an accident. Years ago, when we were just babies. They flipped our truck. Rolled down a bank coming back from the lake. They were drinking. My dad was driving. He died instantly. My uncle Billy, he's Clayton's dad, and my mom were pinned. It took three days to find them. My uncle died the night before they were found. My mom watched her twin brother die. And she was pinned beside my dad. For three days.

SAM

Oh my god.

MARIE

She almost died too. That's why she limps. She has … a lot of scars. She hurts. Nan and Pa raised the three of us kids. And my mom, she –

SAM

She's a survivor.

MARIE

Yeah.

SAM

And so are you.

> *MARIE and SAM embrace. They kiss.*
> *JOHN has been watching. He enters to*
> *talk to MARIE.*

JOHN

Listen, I just wanted to say –

MARIE

I can't believe you're joining the army.

JOHN

I just wanted to say –

MARIE

You're such an idiot!

JOHN

And what are you? A genius? Everything you think is right, and everything anybody else thinks is bullshit. I came out here to tell you that it's fine that you're gay. That we all support you no matter what. But you're too fucking self-righteous to even hear that.

MARIE

I just think you should –

JOHN

What?! Are you going to tell me how I should live my life now?! You listen for once! You didn't shut up for the whole goddamn dinner. We could barely get a word in edgewise and when we did you'd just shit all over us with your stupid fucking opinions. The only thing you care about is the sound of your own voice and your bleeding-heart bullshit. Sorry I ruined your big coming-out party. You probably thought everyone would be shocked and horrified that you're gay. But guess what? Nobody fucking cares. I hope you're happy. But I doubt it.

JOHN walks away and exits.

MARIE

Oh yeah, big soldier! Walking away from his little sister!

SAM
I thought you two were twins.

MARIE
By five minutes.

SAM
You okay?

MARIE
I'm worried about him.

SAM
Maybe he'll join the Reserves. Be a weekend warrior like my brother was.

MARIE
Your brother's in the army? Why don't I know that?

SAM
Matt. He's in the Reserves.

MARIE
How ironic.

SAM
It's not that weird, actually.

MARIE
Yeah. I know. I just reject it. All of it. Like fucking why? Fighting over some other people's homelands so we can mine it or put a pipeline through it.

SAM
Maybe he just needs structure, or something.

MARIE
Excuse me?

SAM
It's pretty normal, really.

MARIE
Normal?

SAM
Yeah. Normal. It's human. Art and war. It's what we do.
Create and destroy.

MARIE
I don't even know who you are right now.

SAM
Maybe it will be good for him.

MARIE
Are you just playing devil's advocate or something?

SAM
The army is a kind of career. He can pick up a lot of skills
there. That don't have to do with killing people.

MARIE
How can you even say something like that –

SAM
Maybe he'll learn a trade?

MARIE
If he wants to learn a fucking trade, he should learn to
build houses, not bomb them.

SAM

I hear you. Babe. I get it. I'm just saying. I think he's just
trying to be responsible. You know. And this is what he
thinks is right. For him.

MARIE

The world doesn't need another stupid soldier.

SAM

I don't know. Somebody has to fight the genocides.

MARIE

Are you kidding me right now?! When have they ever
fought against genocide? Rwanda, they just watched.
South Sudan ... they just watch.

SAM

Sometimes just watching is all it takes to keep it
from happening.

MARIE

Yeah well what about the genocides here?! Whose
watching that?

SAM

I didn't mean –

MARIE

Why is he fighting for them?

SAM

Maybe he's trying to fight for us?

MARIE

Bullshit!

SAM

Listen, my eldest brother Daryl is a cop. I'm proud of him.
I think he's serving his country. I think it's service.

MARIE

Is a soldier any different than a cop? When Native people
stand up, when there is an uprising? Who do they send
in to keep us in check? The police and the army. So your
brothers can fuck off too!

SAM

Hey. I'm proud of my brothers. When things were hard,
they were there for me. Always. It was hard for my family
too you know. It's like we're always the outsider. Even
when we've been here for three generations. But my family
worked hard and made it work for them.

MARIE

Exactly. You're a settler. So this country is like a great
big apple to you. A great big RED juicy apple. But me?
I am the apple!

SAM

Is that like how I'm a banana?

The moment hangs.

I'm so high right now.

MARIE

The pot brownie?! I'm not feeling it.

SAM

I went into a time warp when I was talking to Pa about
his dog trauma.

MARIE
  He let you call him Pa?

SAM
  Yeah.

MARIE
  Wow. You're in.

SAM
  I am? Hard to tell with this family.

MARIE
  Sam. I'm sorry.

SAM
  I know. It's okay.

          They hug.

MARIE
  Want to go check out the bear?

SAM
  Gross.

SCENE 19: MEAT

Lights up on CLIFFORD. He's standing in front of the turkey carcass. He is stripping meat off the carcass and putting it in storage containers. As he peels the meat off the bones, NAN comes into the kitchen.

CLIFFORD
Gonna make a soup out of this carcass?

NAN
Yeah.

CLIFFORD
Good. What should I do with that bear? Lot of meat there.

The question hangs.

NAN
Should have thought about that before you pulled the trigger.

CLIFFORD
I coulda just left it there you know! But I didn't. It's just a bear! What in hell is the big goddamn deal? There are literally hundreds of them out there. I can make some good money out of it. I can sell that hide. Cape it out nice and clean and it'd make a nice rug. Make some money there for sure. I know a guy.

Beat.

That goddamn Sue. I told her the last time not to come around here if she's going to be stoned like that. Did you see her? I don't know why you coddle her like you do. She's a grown woman. Acting like a goddamn child. If she were my kid, boy I'd straighten her out. Cut her off. That's the only way. Tough love. Otherwise it's just take, take, take. She'll wind up in an early grave. Just like her old man. Useless. Useless.

NAN watches CLIFFORD working away at the turkey. Lights down on NAN and CLIFFORD.

SCENE 20: RESPECTS

MARIE and SAM approach the Bear Mother hanging in the backyard. SAM, terrified and disgusted, is clinging to MARIE.

SAM
Oh-my-god-oh-my-god-oh-my-god.

MARIE is in awe of the Bear Mother, the story Nan told her about their ancestry weighing on her mind.

Oh my god what are you doing?!

MARIE is calm. She takes out a cigarette. Holds it in her hands reverently.

SAM
What's that?

MARIE

Tobacco. I need to ... make her an offering.

> *MARIE lays down her tobacco. She then
> stands. She reaches out and touches the
> Bear Mother.*

I'm sorry.

SCENE 21: GRAVE

> *CLAYTON and SUE are standing at a
> graveyard. They have a beer and a plate of food.
> SAM and MARIE are illuminated as well, but
> they are still in the backyard. SUE places the
> paper plates onto a couple rocks.*

SUE

There you go. Mom made a great dinner. You would have
loved it. The kids are all grown up now. You wouldn't
believe how grown up they are. Marie is so smart. John is
so strong and sure of himself.

CLAYTON

What about me?

SUE

Clayton is good too.

> *SUE stands and CLAYTON joins her. He puts
> his arm around her. He takes his beer bottle,
> raises it in a toast, and pours some beer out
> onto the ground.*

CLAYTON

Miss you guys. Miss you so much.

SUE *comforts CLAYTON, who clings to her.*

SUE

Hey. It's okay. It's okay. Oh. There, there, it's okay. You
make them proud. You remind me so much of your dad.

CLAYTON

Yeah?

SUE

Yeah.

CLAYTON

Thank you for saying that.

> *CLAYTON looks at her. SUE caresses the*
> *back of his neck lovingly. She kisses him on*
> *the forehead. CLAYTON looks into her eyes.*
> *CLAYTON kisses SUE on the lips. SUE pulls*
> *away from him. SUE places her finger on his*
> *lips and shakes her head, but says nothing.*
> *SUE leaves CLAYTON by the grave site, lost*
> *and confused.*

> *Transition to:*
> *CLIFFORD sitting in his chair under his*
> *trophy heads. He is struggling a bit. There*
> *is pain in his chest. He takes out a large pill*
> *bottle and takes his medication with a shot of*
> *whiskey. He settles.*

Transition to:
JOHN standing in the kitchen. He takes the
bear heart out of the bloody plastic bag and
bites into it. He swallows the heart of the
Bear Mother.

Transition to:
NAN standing before the gutted bear. It hangs
like a vanquished giant.

Transition to:
SUE, very intoxicated, staggering down
centre stage. The BEAR DANCER charges
in slow motion toward SUE. They dance as
though SUE were being attacked by the BEAR
DANCER. The BEAR DANCER dances SUE
to the ground.

Blackout.

End of Act One.

Act Two

SCENE 1: WAR

Lights up on JOHN in his fatigues. He is dirty
and looks tired. He is recording a selfie video.

JOHN
Hi. It's been a while since I sent a video. It's hot.
Fifty degrees the other day. Crazy heat. But I'm okay.
Sometimes the kids around here run up to us. Some of
the guys are paranoid, thinking they're going to suicide-
bomb us or toss a grenade or something, but they're just
looking for treats or money or whatever. One of the guys
shakes up this can of pop and tosses it at them. It sprayed
all over their faces. It was funny. The kids all laughed.
It was cute. Then one of the guys decides it would be fun
to toss a concussion grenade at them. To ring their bell,
he says. This kid picks it up thinking it was another treat,
and ... Boom.

> *Beat.*

Blew his little fingers off. Almost killed him. There was a
big shit storm.

> *JOHN stops filming the video.*

Fuck. I can't send that.

> *JOHN deletes the video and starts a new one.*

> *Transition to:*
> CLAYTON *and* CLIFFORD *arguing.*

CLAYTON

Conservation Officers came and asked me a bunch of
questions. About bear parts.

CLIFFORD

What did you tell them?

CLAYTON

What do you think I told them? I said I had no idea what
the hell they were talking about. Which means I lied to
them, which means if they come knocking on your door
because they busted that Chinaman you sold those bear
parts to, you better not tell them I was there!

Transition to:
JOHN recording another video. ·

JOHN

Hi Nan. Pa. Just sending you a video to say I miss you
guys. Hope you have an awesome Thanksgiving. Say hi
to Clayton and Mom. I'm thinking of you all. I'm doing
good. When you see Marie, tell her to shut up. Love
you guys. Bye.

JOHN stops filming. Lights down on JOHN.

Transition to:
Lights up on MARIE giving a lecture on
violence against nature and how it relates to
violence against women.

MARIE

My thesis, which I am defending here today, is that the
violence we see against women within our societies is

linked inextricably to violence committed against the land and the natural world.

Lights up on SUE at a 12-step meeting. She stands up to speak.

SUE

Hi, my name is Sue and I'm an addict. I've been sober now going on eight months?

MARIE

The deterioration of the natural world vis-à-vis resource extraction and the commodification and exploitation of wildlife is directly linked to the exploitation, commodification, and abuse of Indigenous women's bodies.

SUE

Everyday can be a struggle just to get by. It's not just the physical pain, it's the pain, in here too. Inside. I think what I really need is to heal. I have a lot ... a lot of things that happened. That I buried. I thought I buried so deep. But now, it's all coming up. It's all bubbling up to the surface. And I'm remembering. I'm remembering when my father died. And I'm remembering when ... my stepfather came into our lives.

Transition to:
NAN, CLAYTON, and CLIFFORD arguing.

CLIFFORD

You and John have a status card. You can claim the bears and then they can't say squat!

NAN

That doesn't make any sense!

CLAYTON

Is that what you brought me for? Cover?

CLIFFORD

You showed me where to find those goddamn bears at the Stink Farm. You're in as much shit as I am.

NAN

What is wrong with you two! What were you thinking?

CLIFFORD

If I get nailed for this, we'll lose everything. I'll lose my guns, my truck. We'll lose the house. Everything!

Transition to:

MARIE

The marginalization of Indigenous communities within capitalist societies is not just a byproduct of colonization but a necessary project toward the success of industry and enterprise within the colonized state.

SUE

I am remembering things, that I don't want to remember. About him.

MARIE

The erosion of the Indigenous family in this light is not just a product of a fraught history –

SUE

And me.

MARIE

– but a deliberate and necessary assault undertaken by the colonizer in the objective pursuit of dominance over the land and its resources.

> *Transition to:*
> *CLIFFORD giving a statement to*
> *Conservation Officers. He has been charged*
> *with poaching and selling animal parts.*

CLIFFORD

Actually, I brought those boys with me. I think it was actually Clayton who shot those cubs. But he's ... In – First Nations. So, you know. Native Rights. Right?

MARIE

Environmental chauvinism is embedded within patriarchal societies. And until the patriarchal structure is uprooted and replaced by systems more firmly rooted in the central role of the feminine, unsustainable environmental degradation is inevitable.

NAN

He did it for me. He took those bears for me, your Honour. My family. We come from the Bear. The Bear gives us gifts.

MARIE

Indigenous matriarchal societies value the female body, and by that virtue the health of the natural world.

NAN

In the old days, the Bear gave us songs.

MARIE

If we are going to survive in the face of rapid
environmental collapse we must first embrace
the feminine.

NAN

My mother knew all the plants of our Territory. She
told me that it was the Bear who taught our family how
to use the plants. How to use the medicines. The Bear
is medicine.

MARIE

We must embrace the feminine, and by doing so, offset the
colonial patriarchy.

SUE

I have to face him. I don't want to, but I have to be brave.
And strong. I choose this path to stay clean for myself.
I want to be strong for my family.

> *MARIE and SAM are talking to NAN on
> the phone.*

NAN

How are you doing? How is school going?

MARIE

I just defended my thesis! I'm vibrating! I feel like I can
do anything!

NAN

Oh? That's nice dear.

MARIE

I want babies!

SAM and NAN
  What?!

SAM
  You just finished school. Can't we just bask in
  the afterglow?

NAN
  How are you two going to have babies?

MARIE
  I don't know. Still got that old turkey baster?

NAN
  Oh you! I'm going now. You're getting gross.

        *NAN hangs up on them and turns to face
        CLAYTON and CLIFFORD, who sits in his
        chair drinking whiskey.*

CLAYTON
  You know what we're facing? Five years. Five fucking years.
  And a $250,000 fine! I hope it was worth it. I hope it was
  fucking worth it.

NAN
  How could you be so stupid? How are we going to pay
  for that? I got up there and said I wanted you to kill those
  bears for me. But all I wish is that you didn't murder
  them for money!

CLIFFORD
  Just shut up.

NAN

You knew where to find her because of my story. I told you the story of how she charged at me in the berry patch. And you remembered. And you went up there and killed her and her cubs.

CLIFFORD

Yeah. I did.

NAN

I told the judge you did it for me.

CLIFFORD

I did! That money fed us, put fuel in my truck, and paid for the electricity.

NAN

I lied for you.

CLIFFORD

You didn't help anything. Telling them that bears are medicine. You know what my Chinese buyers use bear parts for?! Medicine!

NAN

What are we going to do?

CLAYTON

I know what we're going to do. Old man here is going to jail. Me too, probably!

CLIFFORD

Shut up.

CLAYTON

If we just shot the bears, no big deal. But you had to go
and carve them up and sell the parts on the black market.
I told you where to find those other bears hanging around
the Stink Farm so now I'm caught up in it. And you never
even gave me a cut! Cheap bastard!

NAN

How long you been doing that anyways? How many other
bears you sell?

CLIFFORD

I said shut up!

NAN

There's nothing stopping what's coming now. There's
nothing I can do to stop it.

> *CLAYTON exits.*
> *CLIFFORD sits in his chair. NAN stairs at*
> *him a moment and then exits.*
> *SUE enters. She stands in silence*
> *watching CLIFFORD.*

CLIFFORD

What the hell do you want?

> *SUE is stealing herself to speak, but*
> *remains quiet.*

Well? What the hell do you want? I don't have any money
for you to get high on, okay?! I don't have anything left to
give to this goddamn family! Alright?! I gave you people
everything! Everything I had! And are you grateful?! Are
you?! No! You just take, take, take!

SUE
I remember.

CLIFFORD
What?

SUE
I remember.

CLIFFORD
What are you talking about?

SUE
I remember you, being drunk. When we were kids. And one time, coming into my room. Into my bed. I buried it. But … I remember now.

CLIFFORD freezes.

CLIFFORD
I don't … I don't know what you're talking about. You were just a kid, I would never –

SUE
But you did.

CLIFFORD
I would never … Sue. That was a long time ago. I would never hurt you –

SUE
But you did. I remember.

CLIFFORD
You don't know what the hell you're talking about!

CLIFFORD exits. SUE exhales the darkness.

Transition to:
The BEAR DANCER appearing upstage
centre. CLIFFORD appears downstage.
He is clutching his rifle. Faced with the reality
and the consequences of what he has done,
CLIFFORD breaks down. The animal trophy
heads above the mantle turn to look down at
CLIFFORD. He sees the heads looking at him.
He falls to his knees clutching his rifle. The
BEAR DANCER opens her transformation
mask, revealing a gaping bear skull interior.

Blackout.
Gun shot.

End of Act Two.

Act Three

SCENE 1: GATHERING

SUE is on the phone with JOHN.

SUE
When are you coming?

*CLAYTON enters carrying the box holding
CLIFFORD's ashes.*

SUE
Okay. Good. Be safe.

SUE hangs up.

CLAYTON
Where's Nan?

SUE
Sleeping.

CLAYTON
That John?

SUE
Yeah. He should be here tonight. Can he stay
at your place?

CLAYTON
Okay.

SUE
The girls will be here tonight. So keep it calm. For Nan.

CLAYTON
O' course.

SUE
Someone needs to make the fire. You're the fire watcher.

CLAYTON
I can do that. How do I do that?

SUE
Make a fire in the fire pit.

CLAYTON
Okay.

SUE
I'm going to check on Mom.

> *SUE exits.*
> *CLAYTON gets a bottle of whiskey and a glass*
> *out of Clifford's liquor cabinet and approaches*
> *the wooden box containing Clifford's ashes*
> *over to the mantle. He places the glass under a*
> *picture of Clifford that hangs on the wall like a*
> *portrait of a monarch. He pours some whiskey*
> *into the glass as an offering to Clifford, then*
> *takes a drink from the bottle.*

CLAYTON
Jesus Christ, Pa. Guy faces five years in jail and a quarter-million-dollar fine and he just ups and kills himself. Pretty fucking convenient if you ask me. Pretty fucking convenient. They're coming after me now. Like I was the mastermind of the whole thing. And Nan has to pay your fine. She probably has to sell the house. Idiot. Where the

fuck is she going to live? What do you care? You're dead. Dust. (*pause*) History.

> *CLAYTON exits.*

SCENE 2: REUNION

> *NAN enters, and goes over to Clifford's portrait. She puts her hand on the box containing his ashes.*

NAN
All of you fits inside that little box now.

> *CLIFFORD enters, dressed as he is in the portrait hanging on the wall. NAN turns to see him standing there looking at her.*

What are you doing here?

CLIFFORD
One last powwow?

> *CLIFFORD crosses to NAN; they slow dance. CLIFFORD twirls NAN and exits. NAN watches him as he exits. JOHN enters, dressed in military uniform. NAN turns to see him.*

NAN
What are you doing here?

JOHN

I'm here for you.

NAN

You look like you've walked a thousand miles.

JOHN

I have.

NAN

You look handsome in your uniform.

JOHN

Thanks.

> *JOHN crosses to NAN and embraces her.*
> *JOHN leads NAN offstage.*

SCENE 3: WAKE

Underscore. ALL are gathered over Clifford's grave, their heads bowed. One by one they pour a handful of dirt on the grave and leave the graveyard. NAN is left with SUE who stands behind her. SUE puts her hand on NAN's shoulder as she leads her away from the grave site.

Transition to:
SUE taking care of her family. JOHN, CLAYTON, MARIE, SUE, and SAM gather in the kitchen. NAN sits quietly in the living room in Clifford's chair. SUE, JOHN,

*CLAYTON, MARIE, and SAM move into the
living room.*

JOHN
I really wish I got a chance to say goodbye, you know.

CLAYTON
Yeah. Well soak this place up while you're here. Nan's
probably going to lose the house.

JOHN
What? No!

MARIE
I can't believe he's gone.

SUE
Did Pa ever …

MARIE
What?

SUE
Never mind.

MARIE
What?

SUE
Did he ever do anything to hurt you?

MARIE
What are you talking about?

SUE

Nothing. Never mind.

MARIE

Pa never laid a finger on me. He was just my grumpy
old Pa. He would never lay a finger on me. Nan would
have his ass.

SUE

Of course.

MARIE

I can't believe he's gone. I can't believe he did that. Why
would he do that?

MARIE breaks down. SUE comforts her.

NAN

I think I ... need everyone to go now. I want everyone to
go. There's too many people here, now. I don't want to see
anyone. I don't want ...

SAM

Oh Nan, let me help you.

NAN

What are you doing here? Who are you? Get out.

SAM

I'm so sorry, Nan.

NAN

Get out! I want everyone out!

SUE
  Mom?

NAN suddenly stands up, confused.

NAN
  I want to go home.

MARIE
  What is she talking about? She is home.

NAN
  I just want to go home. I ... I want to go home! Someone
  take me home! Please!

SUE
  Okay. Okay Mom. I'll take you home. I got you.

CLAYTON
  But she is home –

SUE
  It's too much for her. Let's just get out of her way for a bit.

CLAYTON
  Okay, okay.

SUE
  Come on, Mom. Let me help you up. I'll take you to bed.

SUE takes NAN to her bedroom.

MARIE
  We can't be kicked out! I'm pregnant!

> CLAYTON's basement apartment. JOHN
> watches CLAYTON play a war-based
> video game.

CLAYTON
  You kill anyone yet or what?

JOHN
  Fuck. That's like the one question you're not supposed to
  ask a soldier.

CLAYTON
  Why?

JOHN
  Because it's ignorant.

CLAYTON
  Oh. I didn't know. Never hung out with a soldier before.
  You have any war stories?

JOHN
  Can you put something else on?

CLAYTON
  Oh yeah, okay.

> CLAYTON turns the game off and turns on
> the news. War footage is projected onto them.
> JOHN is becoming more agitated.

CLAYTON
You're going to be an uncle! Can you believe it?! I can't.
Like, I really can't. Couple months ago they protested
my work. They were on the roadblock that stopped my
stink truck.

JOHN
Oh.

CLAYTON
Yeah. They cost me. Couple months' work. Still pissed at
them for that. Stupid hippies. (*pause*) Your mom's been
doing good though.

JOHN
Oh yeah.

CLAYTON
No really.

JOHN
Good.

CLAYTON
She's 12-stepping it.

JOHN
Again.

CLAYTON
For real this time.

JOHN
Good.

CLAYTON
  Gotta respect her for trying.

JOHN
  Respect is earned.

CLAYTON
  Right. Sorry. Soldier boy. You have no idea what she has
  been through.

JOHN
  And you do?

CLAYTON
  Yeah. I do. She OD'd. Terry gave her some tainted shit.
  They found her on the side of the road. She didn't want
  anyone to tell you. You know that? Didn't want you to
  worry. Not that you would.

JOHN
  Fuck you.

CLAYTON
  While you were off saving the world I was here. Trying to
  help Nan and Pa. Nursing your mom back to health. And
  now she's sober, and she's trying –

JOHN
  She's been trying my whole life! At some point you just
  surrender and go, "Whatever." Hope you make it through.
  Stick with it. Love you. Don't die.

CLAYTON
  I just said she's doing good.

JOHN
Yeah. I heard you.

CLAYTON
Good.

JOHN
Since when are you her social worker?

CLAYTON
I'm not. I'm family. She's your mom but I love her. I love
her more than you or your sister ever did.

JOHN
Fuck off.

CLAYTON
You two think you're better than everyone else. Me? I ain't
shit, but she was always there for me. And I will always be
there for her.

JOHN
Whatever.

CLAYTON
Whatever?!

CLAYTON *throws a beer can at* JOHN.
They face off.

CLAYTON
You go to war, come back home, and you're still a
little bitch.

JOHN
You know why my mom was always there for
you? Because you're so fucking stupid, your mom
never wanted you!

CLAYTON goes to punch JOHN. JOHN
ducks and CLAYTON misses.

JOHN
Stupid fucking orphan.

CLAYTON charges JOHN, who counters him
and punches him several times. CLAYTON
throws a big punch which JOHN counters
again. JOHN kicks CLAYTON in the groin,
and then knocks CLAYTON out. CLAYTON
falls to the ground. JOHN gets on top of him,
and is about to punch him again but stops
himself. JOHN then gets up off his cousin and
sits on the couch. He turns the TV off. We hear
radio chatter, gun fire and explosions as if from
a long way off. JOHN holds his head, then
settles; finally he sits in silence. CLAYTON
begins to slowly come to. He is dazed and
confused. His head aches.

CLAYTON
You kicked me in the balls. That what they teach you in
the army? Kick them in the balls and beat the shit out of
them when they can't fight back.

JOHN
Yeah.

CLAYTON
You're like Captain America but in reverse. Johnny Canuck.

JOHN
You're such an asshole.

CLAYTON
You kick me in the balls and knock me out in my own house, but I'm the asshole.

JOHN
Yeah. You are.

> CLAYTON *gets up off the ground. He sits*
> *beside JOHN on the couch.*

CLAYTON
I haven't seen you in three fucking years. I was just curious. I just wanted to know what you've been up to. Fuck's sake.

> JOHN *takes a breath.*

JOHN
It's not like a fucking video game.

CLAYTON
It's what you wanted. You wanted to join the army.

JOHN
Yeah.

CLAYTON
I'm glad you made it back. In one piece.

> *Beat.*

JOHN
Yeah.

CLAYTON
Come on; I got to go check on the fire.

> *CLAYTON and JOHN get to up to leave.*
> *JOHN is isolated in a corridor of light.*
> *He walks downstage toward the memory.*

SCENE 5: FIRST KILL

> *JOHN relives the memory of his first kill,*
> *hunting with CLIFFORD. As JOHN tells*
> *the story of the hunt he is downstage looking*
> *into the light corridor that illuminates him.*
> *CLIFFORD, who is centre stage, acts out the*
> *hunt as though he is reliving it.*

JOHN
I was twelve. You got me up early. Four thirty in the morning. Had all my gear ready for me. It was November. Rutting season. There was about a foot of fresh snow out in the mountains. We walked into the wind. To keep our scent behind us. I remember how proud I felt. Like a man. To be a provider. For our family.

CLIFFORD
You hear that?

> *The sound of antlers knocking together in*
> *the distance.*

CLIFFORD
    Two big bucks.

JOHN
    We creep up on them. They're fighting in the willows. The
    brush is shaking back and forth. I'm struggling to keep up.
    Snow is too deep. It's crunchy. Loud.

        The sound of the antlers and hooves stops.

CLIFFORD
    They're gone.

        CLIFFORD glares at JOHN. Furious.

JOHN
    We're going back to the truck. I feel shitty. Like a failure.
    I disappointed you.

        CLIFFORD sees the bucks.

JOHN
    All of a sudden, you freeze. What are you looking
    at? And then –

        CLIFFORD mimes raising his rifle and firing.

    Boom! My ears are ringing. Can't hear a thing. You run up
    to where it dropped.

CLIFFORD
    Damn. It's not the big one.

JOHN
Looks big to me! Its rack is enormous. Thick and strong.
He's a big animal. Still alive. Still breathing. Still looking
around. Still trying to get away.

CLIFFORD
That big bastard he was rutting with is still in here. I don't
want to punch my tag on this one. Do you think you could
have shot it?

JOHN
Yeah.

CLIFFORD
Good. Then it's yours. Anyone asks you, you tell them you
shot it. Okay?

JOHN
Okay.

CLIFFORD
Get your knife out; you have to gut it.

JOHN
Why?

CLIFFORD
Because it's yours.

    Rattles.

JOHN
I look into his eyes. His legs are still kicking. Trying to
get away. He raises his head to look at us. His tongue
flicking in and out.

CLIFFORD
Cut his throat before he gets up.

JOHN
You hold him by the horns. My knife is sharp.

CLIFFORD mimes holding the antlers.

JOHN
I watch his eyes as he bleeds out into the snow.
You feel that?

CLIFFORD
What?

JOHN
Like something left.

CLIFFORD
It's just a thing. Meat. Bone. Hair. Blood.

JOHN
You show me how to gut it. Hide hand, knife hand, don't
switch up. All that.

CLIFFORD
We'll take the liver for Nan. Nan loves her fresh liver.

JOHN
You cut the heart out of the gut pile. You cut a chunk off
and give it to me.

CLIFFORD
Eat it.

JOHN
It's raw.

CLIFFORD
Eat it.

JOHN mimes eating a piece of raw deer heart.

Supposed to make you a good hunter. Drinking the blood.
Eating the heart. That's what Nan says.

*CLIFFORD fades from JOHN's remembrance
and retreats to his chair. JOHN salutes.
We hear the sound of radio chatter, as before.
It's the sound of the war inside JOHN. JOHN's
salute withers. JOHN turns towards the
darkness and exits. SUE enters the living room.*

SCENE 6: FORGIVING THE DEAD

*SUE approaches the wall with Clifford's photo,
the box of ashes, and the animal heads.*

SUE
I remember the first day Mom brought you home. I hated
you. I said –

*CLIFFORD is sitting in his chair. His face is in
shadow. SUE turns to face him.*

CLIFFORD
"You're not my daddy."

SUE

　　And you said –

CLIFFORD

　　No. I'm not your daddy. I could never replace him.

SUE

　　And you never tried to.

CLIFFORD

　　Well. Why would I? But I raised you. All of you. Like you were my own.

SUE

　　You even got our kids, too.

CLIFFORD

　　Well, you couldn't raise them on your own. And Nan would have rather died than have them taken away.

SUE

　　What would we be without you?

CLIFFORD

　　You needed help.

SUE

　　All the times you belittled me. Made me feel stupid and small. Got drunk. Got angry. Got mean. You hurt me.

CLIFFORD

　　It was a long time ago. I was drunk. I don't remember.

SUE

　　I remember.

CLIFFORD
What doesn't kill you makes you stronger. You survived.
Now you're stronger.

SUE
You hurt me.

CLIFFORD
I saved you.

SUE
Did you? Or did we save you?

> *Beat.*

CLIFFORD
You did.

> *Beat.*

SUE
You hurt me.

CLIFFORD
I did.

> *Beat.*

SUE
I ... forgive you.

CLIFFORD
Thank you.

CLIFFORD fades into the shadows. Lights down on SUE.

Transition to:
A special on JOHN centre stage. He is clutching Clifford's rifle. The BEAR DANCER appears up centre. Her mask is open revealing the Bear Skull inside. We hear the sound of the deer antlers rattling and the distant radio chatter and explosions of the war inside JOHN's head.

MARIE enters. She goes into the kitchen and rummages through the fridge. JOHN puts the rifle away, near or on the mantle/shrine. The BEAR DANCER closes her transformation mask and fades away. MARIE notices JOHN in the living room.

MARIE
What are you doing?

JOHN
Nothing.

CLAYTON enters the kitchen.

CLAYTON
Late night snack, cuz?

MARIE
I'm starving. And I'm full.

CLAYTON
I can see that.

JOHN
  You eat meat?

MARIE
  I'm pregnant with twins. I eat everything.

JOHN
  How are you doing?

MARIE
  I'm as big as a whale and I'm about to set sail.

        JOHN laughs.

JOHN
  You carry it well.

MARIE
  Fuck off.

JOHN
  It's good to see ... so much of you.

        MARIE laughs.

MARIE
  Fuck off. It's good to see you too.

        *The two siblings, MARIE and JOHN, hug
        each other, for the first time in many years. It's
        awkward because MARIE is so pregnant.*

  Oh hey, before things get crazy ... check this out.

MARIE gets her phone out, and plays an audio
file. It's a digitized wax cylinder recording of
an Indigenous person singing a Bear Song.

JOHN
What the hell is that?

MARIE
That's our great-great-grandmother. I found it in the
National Archives. She was recorded singing it by an
ethnographer over a hundred years ago. I found it when I
was trying to help Nan with the court case. She's singing a
song for twins. A song given to our family by the Grizzly
Bear. This is our song.

MARIE, JOHN, and CLAYTON listen to
the song.

CLAYTON exits the kitchen. Lights fade
on MARIE and JOHN as they listen to the
Grizzly Bear Song.

CLAYTON enters the living room where SUE
is sitting strumming her guitar.

CLAYTON
Hey.

SUE
Hey Clay.

CLAYTON
How're you doing?

SUE
  I'm good.

CLAYTON
  Yeah?

SUE
  Yeah. How 'bout you? How are you doing?

CLAYTON
  Ah hell. Typical. Up shit creek. Forgot my paddle.

SUE
  Hey. We'll get through this. All of it.

        SUE reaches out and takes CLAYTON's hand.

CLAYTON
  Yeah. Maybe.

        NAN enters.

CLAYTON
  I got to go check on the fire.

        CLAYTON exits.

SUE
  It's late, Mom.

NAN
  Can't sleep. Where is everyone?

SUE
  You kicked them out. Remember?

NAN

No I didn't. Why would I do such a thing?

SUE

Can I get you anything?

NAN

No.

NAN sits down on a chair.

NAN

You know, you live your life. Day in and day out. Same
old same old. And then one day it just flips on you.
Everything. All the work you put in. All the worry. All the
hope. And you're just left. Lost.

SUE

We'll get through this. We always do.

NAN

And then what? Where do we go from here? I'm going to
have to sell the house, the property. There's no other way
to pay Clifford's fine. Your father bought this property
years ago. We could have just lived on the reserve.
He wanted to be independent. But he couldn't let go of
the bottle. Then he died and Clifford came into our lives …
And now … What am I going to do now?

SUE

I'll take care of you.

NAN

How? You can barely take care of yourself.

SUE

   I'm working on it.

NAN

   I know, dear. I'm sorry.

SUE

   I'll take care of you.

NAN

   Got nothing better to do?

SUE

   I want to. I owe you. For all the years you put up with me.

NAN

   I have worried about you my whole life. I still worry about
   you. You're my biggest baby.

> *SUE and NAN sit together. Mother
> and Daughter.*

SUE

   Thank you.

NAN

   For what?

SUE

   Everything. Thank you for giving us everything.

NAN

   That's what mothers do. Sing me a song.

SUE
   Okay.

   SUE plays guitar and sings.

Every day I try to kick you out of my heart. But
your memory keeps dragging me down. I try and
I try, but you hold on so tight. I don't cry, I just
laugh like a clown.

Laugh like a clown, the life of the party. Laugh
like a clown, cover up my heartache.
Laugh like a clown, pick myself, off the ground.

Every day I try to keep the kids in my life. But
the things that I've done let them down. I try and
I try, but I hold on too tight. I don't cry, I just
laugh like a clown.

Laugh like a clown, the life of the party. Laugh
like a clown, cover up my heartache.
Laugh like a clown, pick myself off the ground.

Every day I try to find the light in my life. And
stay away from the trouble in town. I try and I try,
take it one day at a time. Now I cry and I laugh
like a clown.

Laugh like a clown, the life of the party. Laugh
like a clown, cover up my heartache.
Laugh like a clown, pick myself off the ground.
Off the ground.

*As SUE sings, MARIE and SAM enter the
room, drawn by the music. Then CLAYTON
and JOHN enter. As the songs ends –*

MARIE
  My water broke!

SUE
  What?

SAM
  We have to go to the hospital! Now!

MARIE
  They're coming!

SAM
  They're early! NOW people!

CLAYTON
  Let's go! I'll drive you two. John, take your mom.

JOHN
  Okay. Let's go!

SUE
  Oh my god! Okay. Shit.

NAN
  Take the truck. Go on. Go. I'll be fine here.

SUE
  Okay. I'm going to be a grandma! I'm going to
  be a grandma!

*SUE, CLAYTON, and JOHN rush with
MARIE and SAM to hospital, leaving
NAN alone.*

SCENE 7: LEGACY

*Distant music. A corridor of light appears, and
NAN slowly gets up and walks down it. She
turns to look back and sees:*

*SAM, MARIE, and SUE enter. MARIE sits
in Clifford's chair. MARIE and SAM are
each holding a baby. Twins! SAM passes a
child to SUE. SUE cradles the baby in her
arms. JOHN and CLAYTON enter. They pass
the babies around. MARIE passes a baby to
JOHN. Lights fade down on them.*

*NAN hears her mother's Bear Song from a
long time ago. The BEAR DANCER enters.
She dances down to NAN. She is without her
mask, revealing the beautiful face of NAN's
ancestor. She faces NAN and they dance
as matriarchs together. NAN's light fades
and the Great Grizzly Bear Mother dances,
in celebration of her legacy.*

Blackout.

End of Play.

PLAYWRIGHT'S ACKNOWLEDGMENTS

I am forever grateful to The Arts Club Theatre for supporting the writing of *Thanks For Giving* and enabling me to direct its initial production. The play was made possible by The Arts Club Theatre Silver Commissions Project. I would particularly like to thank Bill Millerd and Rachel Ditor for their support throughout this process.

I would also like to thank everyone else involved in the initial production of Thanks for Giving: Angela Beaulieu, čaačumḥi – Aaron M. Wells, James Coomber, Rachel Ditor, Leslie Dos Remedios, Tai Amy Grauman, Jeff Harrison, Margo Kane, Tom McBeath, Samantha McCue, Andrea Menard, Ted Roberts, Shyama-Priya, Deneh'Cho Thompson, and Colleen Totten.

Additional thanks to Albert Adams, Gavan Cheema, Ron Dean Harris, Lindsay Lachance, Freda Loring, Jody-Kay Marklew, and Veronique West.

NOTE ON BEAR SONGS

The sound design for the original *Thanks for Giving* production used the following wax cylinder recordings found in the collection of the Canadian Museum of History:

Tetlenitsa, Chief, vocalist. "Cradle song." Obtained by Chief Tetlenitsa in dream. Recorded in 1916 by James Alexander Teit during the visit of an Interior Salish delegation to Ottawa. VI-M-49 (Q), continued on VI-M-50 (Q), on Thompson Music and Linguistics. CCFCS Bobine NO. 10, VI-M-49 to VI-M-72. James Alexander Teit collection. Transferred from wax cylinder to magnetic tape by Eugène Arima in 1961. 72-1062.

XwEli'nEk, vocalist. "Twin song" (really grizzly bear song). Recorded in 1916 or 1918 by James Alexander Teit. VI-M-122 (88) on Thompson Music and Linguistics. On CCFCS Bobine NO. 13, VI-M-121 to VI-M-146. James Alexander Teit collection. Transferred from wax cylinder to magnetic tape by Eugène Arima in 1961. 72-1065.

Yiopatko, vocalist. "Cradle song." Recorded in 1918 by James Alexander Teit. VI-M-212 (Q) on Thompson Music. CCFCS Bobine NO. 16, VI-M-198 to VI-M-219. James Alexander Teit collection. Transferred from wax cylinder by Eugène Arima in 1961. 72-1068.

Photo: Ian Redd

Kevin Loring is the first-ever Artistic Director of Indigenous Theatre at the National Arts Centre of Canada. An actor, director, producer, and playwright, Kevin is a graduate of Studio 58 and of Full Circle First Nations Performance's Ensemble Training Program. He was a Playwright-in-Residence and a company member of the English Theatre Ensemble at the National Arts Centre. He co-wrote, co-produced, and co-hosted the award-winning feature-length documentary *Canyon War: The Untold Story*. He is a recipient of the 2009 Governor General's Literary Award for *Where the Blood Mixes* and the 2010 Governor General's Performing Arts Award's Mentorship Program Prize. Loring is also the founder and Artistic Director of Savage Society, a not-for-profit production company dedicated to telling Indigenous stories sourcing myths, traditions, and the contemporary Indigenous experience. Kevin is N'lakapamux from the Lytton First Nation in British Columbia.